WARBIRDS ILLUSTRATED No 44

Cover illustration: When second-hand CF-104 Starfighters became available in the early 1970s, Denmark purchased outright fifteen CF-104s and seven CF-104Ds from the Canadian government to enable both *Esk 723* and *726* to be brought up to a more realistic strength. The Danes also brought these airframes up to 'G' standard, which included the fitting of Martin-Baker ejection seats in place of Lockheed C2s. The photograph shows the former CF-104D RT-660, from *Esk 726*, in company with F-104G R-345, landing at RAF Coningsby in October 1982. (Author)

1. (Half-title page) *JBG 34* at Memmingham will be the last front-line Starfighter unit in Germany and is not scheduled to relinquish the type until the end of 1987. Seen here high over Bavaria is a four-ship formation of home-produced F-104s,

including 2301, one of the last aircraft to receive a major overhaul by MBB at Manching and resplendent in the new 'lizard' colour scheme. (Hans J. Schroder)

2. (Title spread) The Canadians tried several colour schemes before the demise of the F-104 in CAF service, starting with natural metal and following with overall olive drab and finally olive drab upper surfaces and light grey undersides. Depicted on this AETE-based CF-104 is the first camouflage scheme, this particular aircraft being the first to receive it. The repainting of the fleet took a long time, however, and in fact at no point was there a completely standard scheme in existence. Aircraft 104895, seen here firing CRV.7 rockets, is reported to have been lost on 19 March 1964. (Canadian Armed Forces)

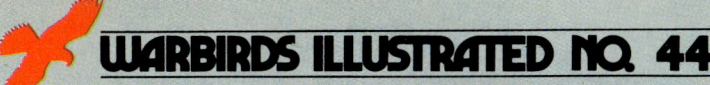

WARBIRDS ILLUSTRATED NO. 44

F-104 Starfighter

PETER R. FOSTER

ARMS AND ARMOUR PRESS

Introduction

First published in Great Britain in 1987 by Arms and Armour Press Ltd., Link House, West Street, Poole, Dorset BH15 1LL.

Distributed in the USA by Sterling Publishing Co. Inc., 2 Park Avenue, New York, NY 10016.

Distributed in Australia by Capricorn Link (Australia) Pty. Ltd., P.O. Box 665, Lane Cove, New South Wales 2066.

British Library Cataloguing in Publication data:
Foster, Peter R.
F-104 Starfighter.—(Warbirds illustrated; 44)
1. Starfighter (Fighter plane)
I. Title   II. Series
623.74'64   TL685.3

ISBN 0-85368-809-5

Edited and designed by Roger Chesneau; typeset by Typesetters (Birmingham) Ltd., printed and bound in Spain by Graphicromo, S.A. Cordoba.

Kelly Johnson and his famous 'Skunk Works' have been responsible for some of the most futuristic aircraft designs ever seen, yet all these incredible machines have been built for a purpose — a purpose which they have fulfilled. The Lockheed F-104 Starfighter is no exception: the fact that it was funded in 1953 and is likely to see service well into the 1990s is, in itself, testimony to its success.

The Starfighter, above almost every other second-generation jet aircraft, holds a special place in my affection. It seems always to have been around during the period of my interest in aviation, although, as a stark reminder of its age, during the 1986 'Tiger Meet' held at Cambrai, France, only two examples of this venerable lady were to be seen; fifteen years ago the Meet would have been dominated by the type. It is with one of the 'Tiger' squadrons No. 439 CAF, that my real feel for the aeroplane was found, and it is to Major Dan Dempsey, who now leads the *Snowbirds* aerial demonstration team, that I shall always be indebted for 1 hour 20 minutes of pleasure when he took me down in the weeds in CF-104D 104650. Out of this sortie came the motivation to produce this portfolio, which is an attempt to record the service use of the Starfighter: through this selection of photographs I hope to be able to share my enthusiasm with the reader whilst constructively describing the 'ups and down' of an aeroplane that even non-aviation minded people have heard of.

For help in compiling this book I am indebted to many friends who have, through their own enthusiasm, contributed so much towards ensuring that a satisfactory photographic record of the aircraft exists. In particular, I owe thanks to Geoff Rhodes for allowing me access to his files, and to several Starfighter operators for their generous help. Finally, it is to Bob Ferguson of Lockheed that we all owe thanks, for ensuring that early examples of all Lockheed's aircraft were recorded for posterity.

Peter R. Foster

◄3
3. The three 1 CAG (Canadian Air Group) units have now converted to the CF-18 Hornet, No. 441 Squadron having been replaced at Baden by No. 409. No. 441 was the last unit to deactivate the F-104, an event which occurred in March 1986. CF-104 104770, flown by Capt. Henry Raffel, is seen here over Bavaria following Exercise 'Jolly Rabbit'. (Author)

▲4 ▼5

4. XF-104 53-7787, seen here high over the Mojave Desert. Along with its sister-prototype, '786, this aircraft was fitted with the Curtiss-Wright J69 engine, which gave 10,500lb static thrust and which was unfortunately to prove, during intensive testing, insufficiently powerful to enable the Mach 2 potential of the airframe to be reached. The first prototype, 37786, flew on 4 March 1954 at the hands of Tony le Vier, and although it was unable to attain more than Mach 0.3 over other US 'Century Series' fighters, the concept of the lightweight fighter was proved. Unfortunately, '787 became the first of many Starfighters to crash; '786 also met an untimely end, in 1957. (Lockheed)

5. YF-104 52956, one of fifteen airframes ordered as follow-ons to the two original XF-104s. These pre-production machines were fitted with the General Electric J79-GE-3 engine, which quickly proved itself capable of pushing the Starfighter to its design limits. Ultimately, some 52 F-104A airframes were to be involved in the flight test programme, flying a total of 8,000 missions. The F-104A was eventually released for service with the USAF in January 1958. (Lockheed)

6. NF-104A 0-60760, now preserved at Edwards Air Force Base outside the AFFTC (Air Force Flight Test Center), was one of three aircraft fitted with a Rocketdome AR-2 rocket motor of 6,000lb thrust in the base of the fin. On 15 November 1963, with Major Robert Smith at the controls, this aircraft gained an unofficial world altitude record of 118,860ft from a ground take-off. The legendary Chuck Yeager, then commander of the Aerospace Research Pilots' School, set out in 60756 in December of the same year to break the record of 113,890ft officially held by the Soviet Union since 1961. Unfortunately, although designed to boost the NF-104 to 140,000ft, the thrusters refused to work at 104,000ft, and Yeager had to abandon the aircraft during the descent because of a frozen stabiliser. (Author)

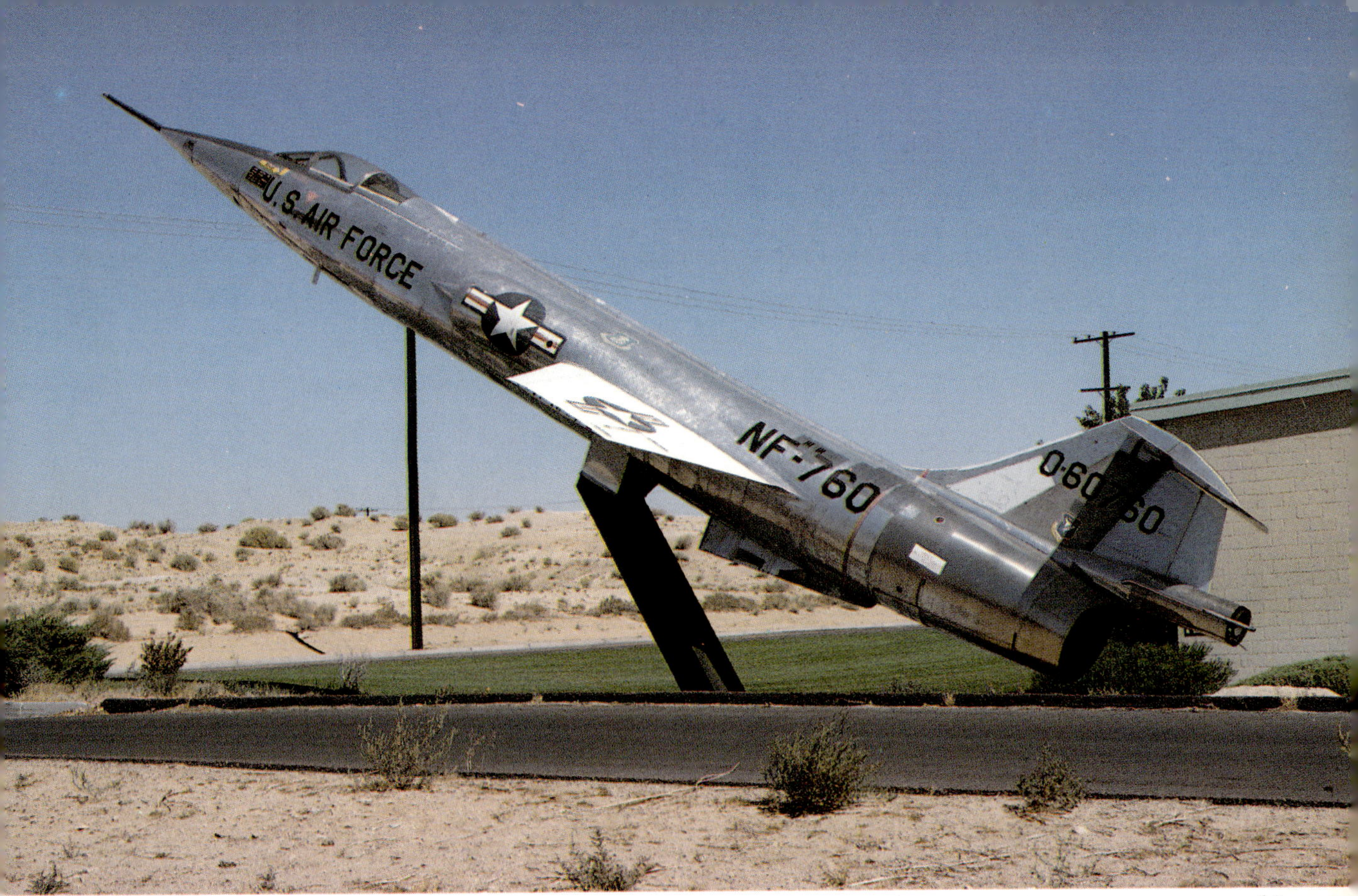

6▲

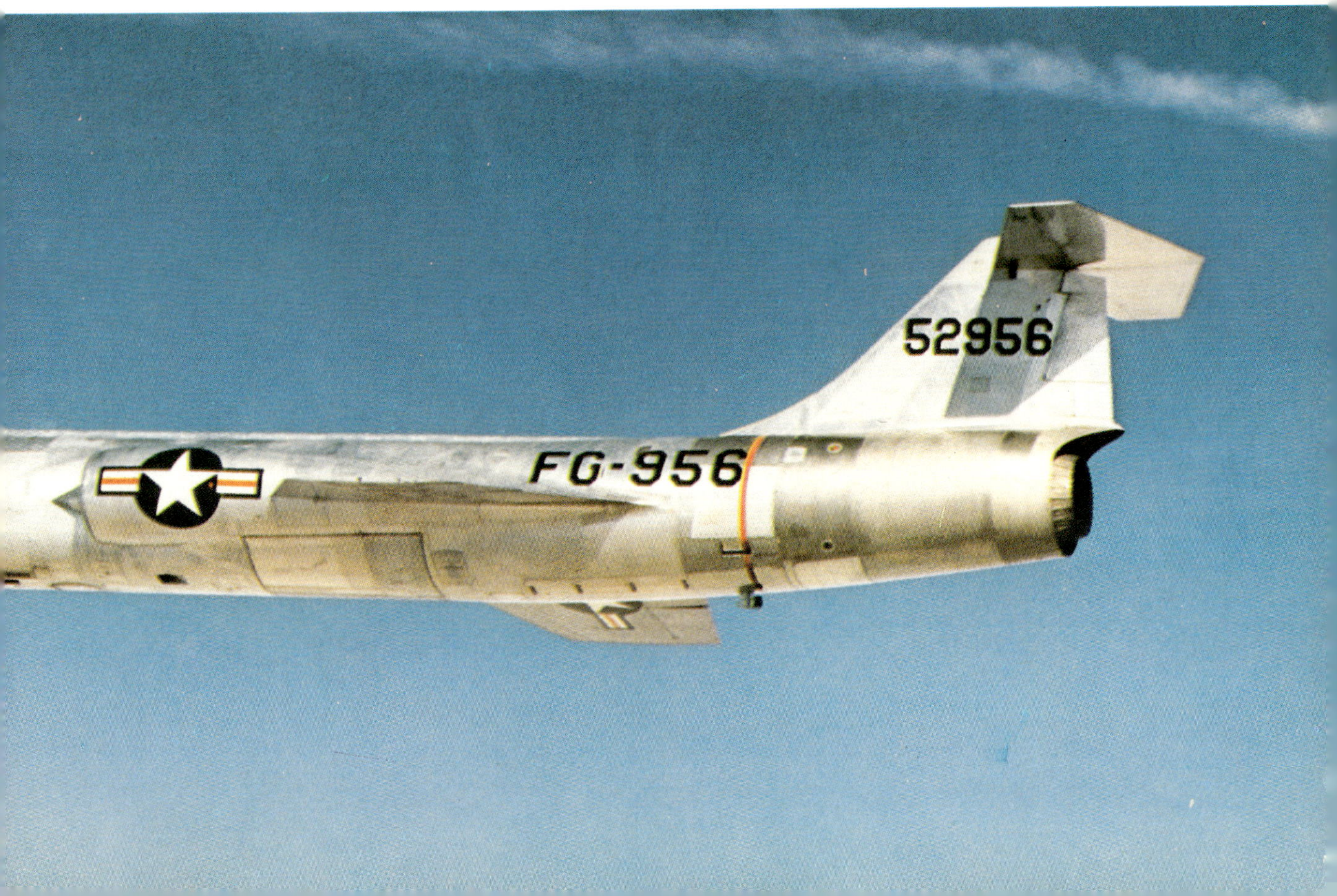

▲ 7

7. The Starfighter entered service with the US Air Force in January 1958, the first recipient being 83 FIS. The F-104A version had first flown in February 1956 and was to set seven climb-to-height records, taking 4 minutes 26 seconds to reach 82,000ft. The example depicted here is 56-0791, photographed while serving with 83 FIS during Project 'Jona' at Hamilton Air Force Base, California. (Via G. B. Rhodes)

8. The F-104A saw very little service with ADC. A number of aircraft crashed (including 60738, 60776, 60792 and 60794), and the type was the subject of a grounding order in April 1958; not surprisingly, the few units operating the -A model were somewhat disenchanted with its reliability. These early variants were withdrawn from the active inventory, and although they were later to equip 319 and 331 FIS, the majority were subsequently passed on to other commands. The example depicted here, 0-60823, formerly of 319 FIS, is shown on the ramp at Davis Monthan Air Force Base wearing the MASDC park code FB038, March 1970. (B. Knowles via G. B. Rhodes)

9. Following ADC's initial rejection of the F-104A, many examples were passed to Air National Guard units, including 157 FIS (South

Carolina Air National Guard), 151 FIS (Tennessee ANG) and 197 FIS (Arizona ANG). F-104B-5-10 57-1301 served with the Arizona ANG and now resides on permanent display at the Florence Air Museum, South Carolina; 60832, also in the picture, was one of the many aircraft lost in the Starfighter's chequered career. (B. Knowles via G. B. Rhodes)

10. Although the regular air force units rejected the F-104A, the type continued to serve with the Air Force Flight Test Center and Test Pilots' School at Edwards AFB for many years, the aircraft shown, 60755, finally being retired in the late 1960s. This particular airframe remained in storage with a dozen or so others until the middle 1970s at Davis Monthan AFB, where it was finally broken up. (Via G. B. Rhodes)

11. The NF-104A eventually gave way to the F-104N astronaut proficiency trainer, but NASA also operated the Starfighter as a chase plane. The agency used various derivatives, NASA 818 depicted here being the former YF-104 55-2961. This aircraft is now preserved at the Smithsonian Institute of Science and Technology, Washington, DC. (Via G. B. Rhodes)

▼ 8

9▲

10▲   11▼

▲12

12. Although a large proportion of the F-104A and -B Starfighter fleet was returned to active service with other non-USAF agencies, 24 airframes were converted into QF-104 target drones, a somewhat ignominious fate only two years after the aircraft's first flight. This photograph of QF-104A 60747, belonging to ADTC at Eglin Air Force Base, Florida, was taken at Eglin in August 1970. (K. Buchanan via G. B. Rhodes)

13. As well as the conversion of 24 airframes to QF-104 standard, deliveries were also made under MAP to non-NATO aligned countries which included Pakistan, Jordan and Nationalist China. The Pakistani aircraft, assigned to No. 9 Squadron, saw action during the 1965 war with India and were the only all-weather aircraft in service with the air arm at that time. This particular airframe, F-104B 57-1309, was one of two dual-control models operated by No. 9 Squadron (the other being 57-1312) and is now preserved at Risalpur Air Base. (L. Peacock)

▼13

14 ▲

14. Pakistan received ten F-104As but lost two on 7 and 17 September during the 1965 war; these were later replaced with aircraft originally supplied to Formosa. The Chinese Nationalists operated a similar number of Starfighters, which equipped No. 28 Squadron located at Ching Chuan Kang Air Base, and the aircraft depicted here, 56-0798, was numbered 4219 before being transferred to Pakistan. It now serves as a monument at Peshawar Air Base. (G. B. Rhodes)

15. The other nation to operate the -A model Starfighter was Jordan, which in 1962 received some eighteen examples to equip one squadron, together with four F-104Bs. The Starfighter unit, No. 9 Squadron, was located at Prince Hassan Air Base and in 1979 re-equipped with the Northrop F-5E. The air defence commitment was then passed to the newly acquired Mirage F.1Cs of No. 4 Squadron at Mafrag-King Hussein Air Base, the surviving Starfighters also being relocated here before retirement. (D. Hughes)

15 ▼

▲16

16. By the time of the initial grounding order, Lockheed had produced a third derivative of the Starfighter, which was to break away from the original concept of a basic interceptor. The F-104C version was delivered to the 831st Air Division in October 1958 and was to see active service with the 479th TFW over a good number of years, being deployed to Torrejon, Spain, and eventually seeing combat in South Vietnam. The F-104C was not very successful, and it was withdrawn from air defence duties because of its lack of radar warning receiver (RWR) equipment and re-directed to tactical operations. In this photograph, 60886, named 'Fannie', is shown as it appeared while deployed to South Vietnam. (D. Menard via G. B. Rhodes)

17. Following service with the 479th TFW the -C and -D models were retired from TAC service, many finding their way into storage at Davis-Monthan. Some airframes, such as F-104D 0-71320 seen here, which went on to serve with 198 TFS, Puerto Rico ANG, languished in the reclamation area until the early 1980s before being finally broken up. (Author)

▼17

18▲

18,19. Other airframes which had served with test establishments were placed in store as possible sources of spares for Starfighter operators, but they were eventually retrieved and now serve as monuments to the past, as can be seen from these two photographs of 60919. Above, the airframe is seen at Davis-Monthan in 1975; in the photo below, taken in 1982, it is proudly displayed on a pedestal at Tyndall Air Force Base as a reminder of its service with ADC. (Author)

19▼

▲ 20

20. The final USAF user of the Starfighter was the 198th TFS, Puerto Rico ANG. Here F-104C 57-0920 is seen high over the Atlantic shortly before the type's retirement from the US Air Force in 1975. The airframe was subsequently preserved at McEntire ANGB. (G. B. Rhodes)

21. In 1958 Lockheed, sensing the need in Europe for a supersonic fighter and with the F-104 production line geared up for a non-existent USAF building programme, managed to convince the West German government of the viability of the Starfighter as a replacement for the ageing F-84s and F-86s then in service. The F-104G, as it was designated, first flew on 7 June 1960 and was to be the major version of the aircraft. The Luftwaffe and Marineflieger had a requirement for some 700 Starfighters to equip twelve units in Germany, but owing to the poor weather in Europe a training programme was set up in the United States to keep pace with the re-equipment schedule. Here Luftwaffe F-104G 13262 is seen landing at Luke AFB, Arizona, in October 1975. (Author)

22. The unit at Luke Air Force Base consisted of the 4512nd, 4518th and 4443rd Combat Crew Training Squadrons (CCTS), and although the aircraft wore USAF markings they were German-owned and operated by German personnel. MAP aircraft were used within the structure to supply initial training for other would-be

users of the Starfighter, including Greece and Turkey, and the first loss to occur within the unit was that of 22312, a Canadair-built MAP aircraft which crashed on 16 May 1965. However, these aircraft were only on strength for a short period. The wing operated up to 112 examples of German-owned Starfighters; the photograph depicts 63-13251, sporting a non-standard red upper surface to the tail. (Author)

23. The unit at Luke Air Force Base became known as *2 Dt. Lw. Ausb. Stff.* and operated a fairly even mix of F-104 and TF-104 aircraft. Unlike the single-seat variants, the dual trainers were all built by Lockheed, although in some instances sub-sections and appendages were supplied by other manufacturers. Depicted here is TF-104 63-8455 overshooting at Luke in October 1981. (Author)

24. As time progressed the output from Luke was decreased and re-structuring took place. The unit, although still run by the Luftwaffe, came under the USAF's 58th Tactical Training Wing and was reduced to two squadrons, 69 TFTS and 418 TFTS. However, shortly before its demise in 1983 this was further reduced to one squadron, 69 TFTS, and seen here is F-104G 63-13269 with the serial number suitably redesigned to reflect the squadron number. This airframe, along with 66 others, was sold by the West German government to Taiwan in 1983. (Author)

▼ 21

22 ▲

23 ▲   24 ▼

▲25

25. The F-104G was to become the standard production model, but in order to assist with the tactical weapons phase the Luftwaffe took delivery of 30 F-104F two-seaters which were basically 'europeanised' F-104Ds. These served almost entirely with *WS 10* at Jever until being replaced by late-model TF-104Gs. The airframes were then retired to various ground roles; several were preserved, including 2902 at Sonthoven and 2909 (shown) at Jever. (G. B. Rhodes)

26. Crews graduating from Luke AFB progressed to the tactical weapons unit at Jever which operated a mix of single- and two-seaters. Until 1968 all Luftwaffe units operated with a letter/number serial system – *WS 10* aircraft at Jever, for example, being prefixed 'BB' – but in 1968 a complete reorganization took place and Starfighters were allocated numbers in the 2001–2921 range. BB-256, seen here in about 1967, was an RF-104G with the gun port faired over. (Joachim Streit)

▼ 26

27. The bulk of *WS 10*'s equipment consisted of two-seat F-104s, all of which were built by Lockheed. This is TF-104G 2703, which also displays the Lockheed construction number 5704 on the fin and was allocated the serial 61-3033 in accordance with the regulation that all Starfighters used at Luke or procured under MAP conditions should bear USAF identification. The photograph was taken on approach to Alconbury on 12 August 1982. (Author)

28. Having graduated through the weapons course with *WS 10*, the crews proceeded to one of the nine operational units. The structure of the Luftwaffe provided one air defence and one reconnaissance wing in the north and the same in the south, with the five tactical units spread in a curve the length of the country. In the north the air defence unit was *JG 71 'Richthofen'*, based at Wittmundhaven and comprising two *Staffeln*. The unit re-equipped with F-104G from the CL.13 Sabre in 1964 and was to continue with the type for ten years before becoming the first unit to convert to the F-4F Phantom. Seen here is F-104G 2421 in *JG 71* markings, next to an F-4F of the same unit. (Kurt Thomsen)

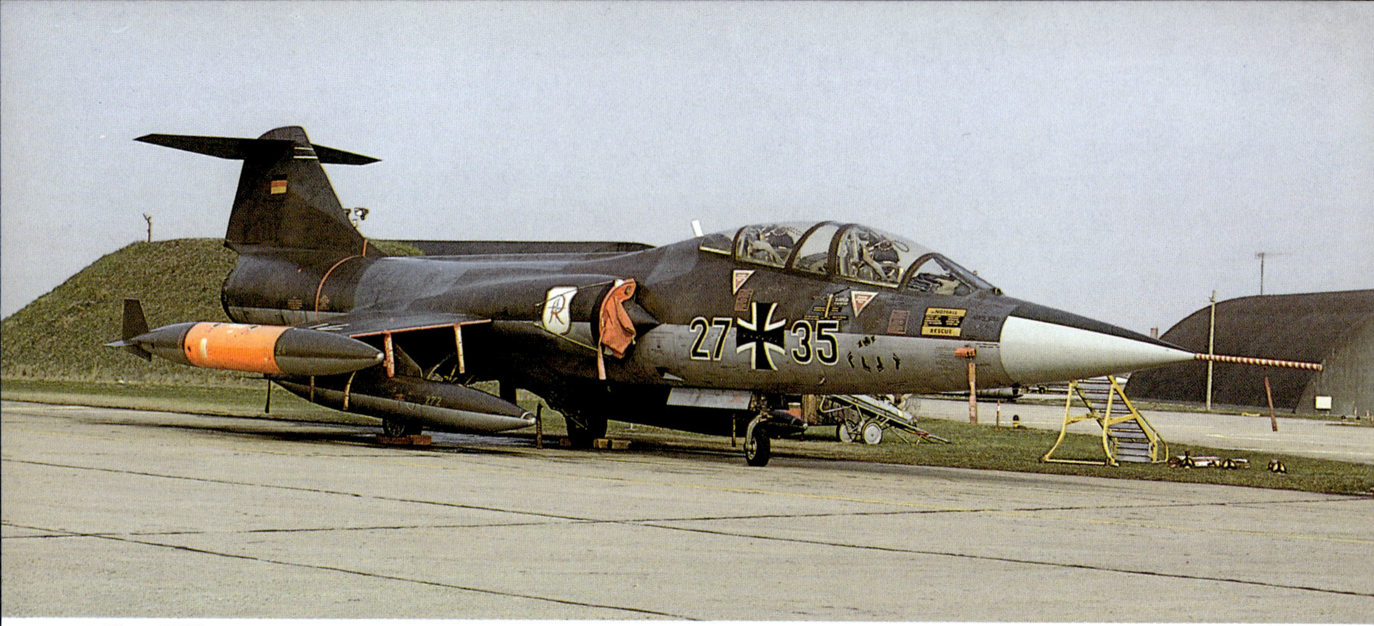

▲29 ▼30

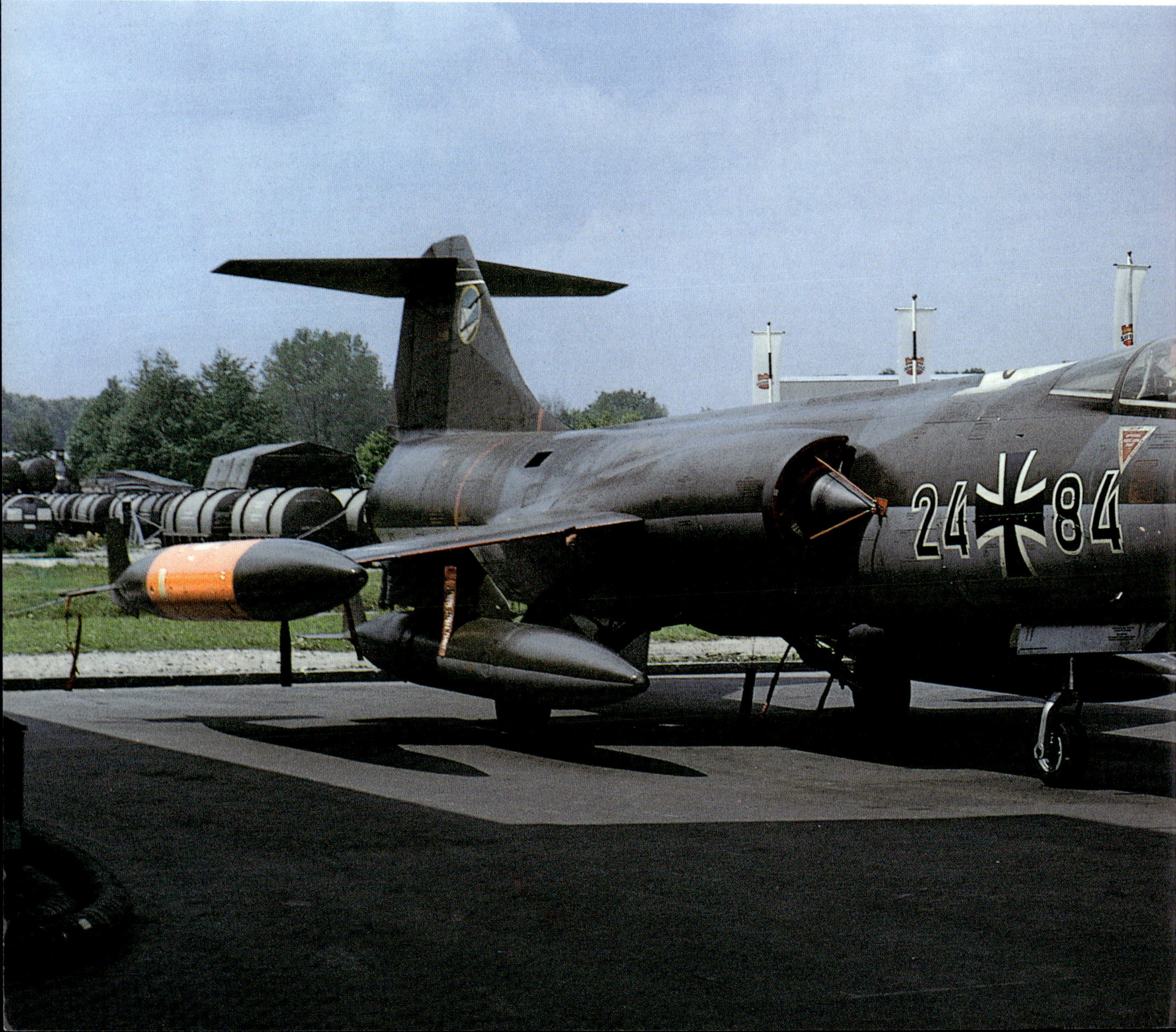

29. Each Luftwaffe unit operated half a dozen TF-104Gs for proficiency rating and check rides: 2735 of *JG 71* is seen here at Nörvenich in March 1974 at the time of its transfer to *JBG 31*. Many F-104s were scrapped when the air defence and reconnaissance units converted to the F-4, although most of the two-seaters were transferred to other units. (Kurt Thomsen)

30. The sister-unit of *JG 71* was *JG 74* at Neuberg, which was identically structured and also passed on to the Phantom in 1974; *JG 74* formed part of 4 ATAF (Allied Tactical Air Force), whilst *JG 71* was part of 2 ATAF. Under the Lockheed Starfighter programme production was set up in Germany, Holland, Belgium, Italy and Canada and the Luftwaffe ended up using a mix of aircraft from the Lockheed, Messerschmitt, SABCA, Fokker and Fiat production lines. Depicted here is 2484, from the Fokker plant at Scipole, having been flown to Erding following *JG 74*'s retirement of the type. (Author's Collection)

31. *Aufklärungsgeschwader 51* formed at Erding in July 1959 with the RF-84F and re-equipped with the Starfighter in 1963, but it was, together with *AKG 52*, to be one of the shortest-lived Luftwaffe F-104 units, flying the type for only about eight years before adopting the RF-4E Phantom. The unit operated F-104s drawn from both Fiat and Fokker converted airframes, although on deactivation these redistributed Starfighters were reconverted for the fighter role; 2392, seen here high over southern Germany, was one so reconverted and is one of the last F-104s in service with *JBG 34*. (Joachim Streit)

▲32

32. *AKG 51*'s sister-unit at Leck in the Flensburg peninsula is *AKG 52*, which was the shortest-serving Starfighter unit. RF-104G 2482, a Fokker-built airframe, is shown here against a setting sun over northern Germany. The reconnaissance package can be clearly seen. (Joachim Streit)

33. *JBG 31* is a frequent visitor to the United Kingdom and is always a prominent participant in annual exercises. This is 2181, photographed at RAF Coningsby during Exercise 'Priory 1/81' in April 1981, which saw service with *JBG 36* before being handed on to *JBG 31* and subsequently to Turkey. *JBG 31* was the first operational unit to adopt the Panavia Tornado. (Author)

34. *JBG 31*'s association with the Starfighter at Nörvenich ended in May 1983 after some twelve years. For the finale, the unit repainted TF-104G 2831 in a special colour scheme based on a design submitted by *Lt.* Herbie Mennen depicting Boelcke, one of Germany's aces and a former member of the unit. On *JBG 31*'s

conversion, 2831 was passed onto *JBG 34* at Memmingham. (Author's Collection)

35. The Luftwaffe, always keen to promote *espirit de corps*, is never slow in presenting special markings when it participates in major NATO events. This Lockheed-built F-104, 2062 of *JBG 32*, is seen at Lechfeld in Bavaria, painted in a colour scheme prepared for a Tactical Air Meet in 1983. The airframe was later to see service with *JBG 33* before becoming one of the many to disappear into obscurity (which generally meant being passed on to Turkey). (Joachim Streit)

36. This Starfighter shows the standard 'splinter' camouflage scheme with 'dayglo' tip tanks, although in the photograph (taken at RAF Leuchars in 1982) 2395 displays a distinctive marking on the luggage pod. This airframe still serves today with *JBG 34* at Memmingham. (Author)

▼33

34 ▲

35 ▲   36 ▼

▲ 37

37. Seen against a mountain backdrop, TF-104G 2725 of *JBG 32* begins its take-off run from Decimomannu, Sardinia, an airfield very well known to Luftwaffe pilots as it is used extensively for weapons training. (Author)

38. F-104G 2062 again, this time with *JBG 33* at Buchel. The aircraft served with the unit for a short period (just over a year) and is portrayed here on a high-level transit to a weapons range, its practice bomblets clearly visible in the dispenser on the centreline station. (Hans J. Schroder)

▼ 38

39. At Buchel, although a base maintenance system exists, attempts at *Staffel* identification have been made with the *JBG 33* badge appearing in either red or blue. Here another Fokker-built F-104, 2533, is seen landing at RAF Honington whilst on exchange with No. 208 Squadron, May 1982. (Author)

40. Very few Starfighters survived to adopt the new tactical colour scheme that began to be applied to Luftwaffe aircraft in 1984, but one of them, 2652 from *JBG 33*, is seen in the 'lizard' scheme whilst taxiing in at RAF Binbrook during Exercise 'Priory 1/85'. It is interesting to note that one *Staffel* had already deactivated for Tornado conversion at this time, the surviving unit adopting a yellow unit badge. (Author)

40▼

▲41

41. The last days of the Starfighter at Buchel provided the excuse for this outlandish scheme on 2167; the design, based on the unit's eagle badge, was perhaps the nicest of the 'farewell' decorations. From the backdrop of undulating countryside it can be understood why, with Germany's inclement weather, Buchel is considered to be one of the more difficult airfields to land at. (Hans J. Schroder)

42. The Luftwaffe's anniversary celebrations brought delightful 'one off' schemes to all manner of hardware, including this deceptive one: the aircraft is painted in the colours of the Federal German flag whilst the 'serial' commemorates the 25th anniversary of *JBG 34* and the 50th of Memmingham. The aircraft is actually 2419, which was originally built as a reconnaissance Starfighter for *AKG 51*. (Hans J. Schroder)

▼42

43 ▲

43. Two-seater 2739 of *JBG 34* in the standard 'splinter' camouflage scheme seen against the green backdrop of RAF Coltishall whilst on exchange with No. 6 Squadron in August 1980. This airframe is another to have spent its entire Luftwaffe career with *JBG 34*. (Author)

44. The final front line Luftwaffe F-104 unit was *JBG 36*. Forming with the Starfighter in 1965, it became, in 1976, the first and only F-104 tactical unit to convert to the F-4F Phantom. The aircraft depicted, 2603, was one of the SABCA-built airframes and went on to serve with *JBG 33* and *JBG 34*. It is shown here in 'clean' configuration whilst displaying at the Lakenheath Open Day in 1973. (L. Peacock)

44 ▼

▲ 45

45. Two Marineflieger units were to adopt the Starfighter for the anti-shipping and reconnaissance roles: based at Schleswig-Jagel and Eggebeck in the Flensberg peninsula, both units, *MFG 1* and *2*, converted from the Sea Hawk to the F-104 in 1965. *MFG 1* later became the first German front-line unit to convert to the Tornado in 1982, whilst *MFG 2* retained its Starfighters until late 1986. Aircraft 2667, depicted here on the flight line at Jagel in 1978, was one of a batch of 50 attrition-replacement airframes produced by MBB at Manching between 1971 and 1973. (Author)

46. One *Staffel* of *MFG 2* operated in the recce role, was predominantly equipped with Fiat-built examples of the Starfighter, and was the last user of the type with the Bundesmarine in 1986. F-104 2124 is seen here during a visit to Alconbury in 1980. (Author)

▼ 46

47. A pair of *MFG 2* F-104s en route to a range facility in Germany. Many ex-German machines have been passed to Greece and Turkey, but it has been mostly ex-Marineflieger airframes that have found their way into service at Araxos with the Royal Hellenic Air Force. (Stefan Peterson via Kurt Thomsen)

48. *MFG 2*'s 'Vikings' were probably the last Starfighter display team. Here 2676 and 2669 await clearance to begin their routine at the Alconbury Air Show in July 1984. During 1985 whilst performing at the IAT display, Fairford, they came very close to passing through the sound barrier right in front of the crowd. (Author)

49. To maintain Starfighter proficiency in Germany, Technical Group 11 (*LVR-1/LW 11*) was formed during 1983. One of its aircraft, 2405, is seen here at the IAT, Fairford. (D. Tuplin)

47▲

48▲ 49▼

▲ 50

50. Germany's trials unit, *Erprobungsstelle 61*, was formed at Manching in 1956 and is used to test all of Germany's military aircraft. It has on strength approximately six Starfighters – including this long-serving example, 2710, seen at Manching in 1979 – and may well be the last user of the F-104. (Joachim Streit)

51. This German F-104 must be one of the most interesting examples of all. Formerly Fokker-built 2391 of *JG 74*, it was retired in 1974 and taken on charge by MBB at Manching, where, converted to a control-configured vehicle and bearing the test serial 9836, it is operated jointly by MBB and *EPB 61*. (Joachim Streit)

▼ 51

52. Having sold the Starfighter to Germany, the process of offering it to other NATO countries (with guarantees of production rights to offset costs) was comparatively easy for Lockheed, and the consortium of European production partners, comprising companies in Holland, Belgium and Italy as well as Germany, was to produce a staggering 1,212 F-104Gs. Fokker in Holland were to build 99 airframes for the Royal Netherlands Air Force and a further 255 for Germany, and the Dutch would also receive 25 from the Fiat line. The RNethAF operated five front-line squadrons plus two conversion units; seen here is D-5804 of CAV at Volkel in 1977. (Author)

52 ▼

▲53

53. No. 306 Squadron Klu (RNethAF) has, throughout its existence, been the only reconnaissance unit within the air force, operating such types as straight-winged F-84E/Gs, RT-33As, RF-84Fs and, since September 1963, RF-104Gs. It became the first Dutch Starfighter unit, with crews that had been trained by the Luftwaffe at *WS 10*. No. 306 was initially the Dutch F-104 OCU, a role it maintained until January 1964 when it re-established its reconnaissance role. (B. Aarts via R. J. Willekens)

54. The two other Volkel-based units were the last to convert to the Starfighter and were employed in the tactical strike role. Centralized servicing introduced within the Klu resulted in the aircraft displaying both sets of unit markings, 311's on the starboard side and 312's on the port. D-8318 is seen here on approach to Volkel in July 1980. (Author)

55. A familiar and nostalgic sight at Volkel with a three-ship, 'burner-lit departure. The aircraft, all from No. 312 Squadron, are a mix of Fiat- and Fokker-built airframes. The serialling system employs aircraft construction numbers, and of those depicted D-6685 was later destroyed in a crash at Erp on 12 October 1978

whilst D-8337 was lost on the Otterburn Range when taking part in Exercise 'Mallet Blow 2/83'. (Author)

56. Participation by Klu units in UK air defence exercises has always been a somewhat 'hit and miss' affair, normally on account of poor weather conditions; there were only two all-weather fighter units in Holland, these being Nos. 322 and 323 at Leeuwarden. A rare treat at Binbrook during Exercise 'Priory 1/81' with clear weather on the wolds was the sight of this 312 Squadron F-104G, D-8312, complete with practice bomb/rocket dispenser on the centreline station. This aircraft was one of the last in service with the Klu, being retired to Ypenburg on 18 October 1984. (Author)

57. The all-weather training and conversion unit (TCA) at Leeuwarden, responsible for all the Klu's air defence pilots, operated eight TF-104Gs. This is D-5702, taxiing out at RAF Coningsby with the Leeuwarden base commander aboard during an annual NATO exchange. D-5702 is a famous Starfighter, having been the Lockheed demonstrator registered N104L before delivery to the Dutch on 30 May 1965. The aircraft was transferred to Turkey on 25 August 1980. (Author)

▼54

55▲

56▲   57▼

▲58

▲59   ▼60

58. 'Parrot Left, Archer Right' — a comment from log books of the past when attempting to define ownership: centralized servicing caused much confusion for enthusiasts for a while. This Fiat-built example, D-6654, is wearing 322 Squadron markings and is seen on the ORP at Leeuwarden. With the introduction of F-16s, shelter space became scarce and the ageing F-104s were left outside. (Author)

59. D-6654, seen from the starboard side displaying No. 323's markings. In this photograph four aircraft are lining up for a 2×2 PI mission, the Sidewinder rails clearly evident on the centreline station. (Author)

60. Towards the end of the Starfighter era in Holland, while F-16 training continued, the remaining F-104s were grouped into a unit staffed by pilots not scheduled for the Falcon programme. The unit was autonomous and displayed an orange badge inscribed 'UFO'

(for *Uit FaserinopOnderdeel*, or phasing-out unit). The unit was only in being for a short period, and one example operated by it was D-8048, seen here at an open day at RAF Lakenheath, Suffolk, just before the aircraft's retirement to Ypenburg in October 1984. (Author)

61. SABCA were to produce 101 F-104Gs and nine TF-104Gs for the Belgian Air Force, to equip four squadrons organized into two wings located at Beauvechain/Bevekom and Kleine Brogel; the requirement was for 100 airframes, but FX27 crashed before delivery and a new airframe, c/n 9082, was produced as a replacement. No. 1 Wing, comprising 349 and 350 Squadrons at Beauvechain, operated in the air defence role and produced one of the great Starfighter display teams, the *Slivers*. F-104G FX23 is seen here at Alconbury during 1975. (Author)

▲62

62. The TF-104Gs were evenly distributed between the two wings, No. 10 Wing at Kleine Brogel comprising 23 and 31 Squadrons. As it is Belgian policy not to sell redundant hardware, most of the surviving F-104s now languish in store at Koksijde, including this Lockheed-built TF-104G, FC02. (Author)

63. Starfighters are noted for their very low approaches, and it pays to observe road traffic signals when they are about. Here FX07, of 10 Wing, just clears the boundary fence at RAF Waddington during Exercise 'Priory 1/80'. (Author)

64. No. 31 'Tiger' Squadron at Kleine Brogel, in common with most other 'Tiger' squadrons hosting the famous meet, suitably doctored their aircraft's colour schemes to represent the theme in 1978. This is FX52. (Author's Collection)

63▲   64▼

65. Apart from the European consortium, two other Starfighter production lines were to emerge, Mitsubishi's Nagoya in Japan and Canadair's at Montreal. Canadair were to produce 200 CF-104s for the RCAF and 140 F-104Gs for the USAF/MDAP scheme. The first CF-104 (as it was designated) was a reworked F-104A, 60770, which had the revised fire control system but not the 'beefed-up' -G model airframe. The initial production aircraft went on to see service with Lockheed at Palmdale and AETE at CFB Cold Lake. Here 104704, bearing AETE's distinctive 'X' marking, is seen over Cold Lake itself. The aircraft today serves as an instructional airframe. (Canadian Armed Forces)

66. Canada operated three wings in Europe as part of its NATO commitment, No. 1 at Marville, France, No. 3 at Zweibrucken, West Germany, and No. 4 at Baden-Söllingen, involving eight squadrons. However, with France's withdrawal from NATO and the banning of all foreign nuclear powers from its country, No. 1 Wing was shut down and the units absorbed into Nos. 3 and 4. The first squadron to convert to the Starfighter was No. 427 at Zweibrucken during December 1962. Here CF-104 104787, in the final colour scheme, is seen landing at RAF Waddington whilst on exchange with No. 29 Squadron. (Author)

67. Following Canada's reduced military commitment in the late 1960s, Zweibrucken was handed over to the Americans and No. 1 Air Division was concentrated at Baden-Söllingen and redesignated 1st Canadian Air Group. 1 CAG then comprised Nos. 421, 439 and 441 Squadrons, the last two having originally been dedicated photo-reconnaissance units. Although this role later changed, 1 CAG continued to maintain at least one aircraft configured with the Vicon recce pod for post-strike missions; 104735, so configured, is seen here from within one of Baden's hardened aircraft shelters (HAS). (Author)

65▶

▼ 66

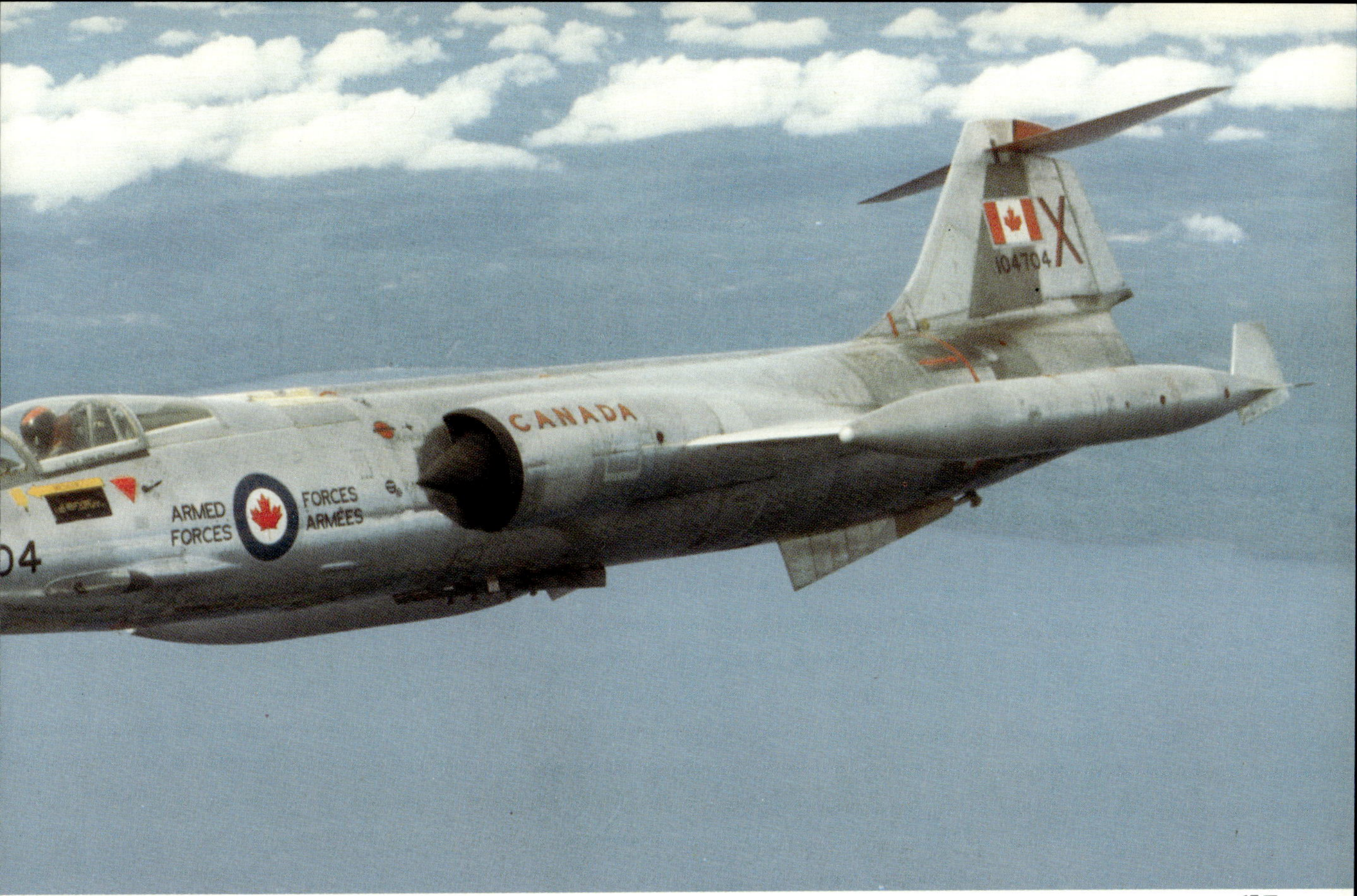

67▼

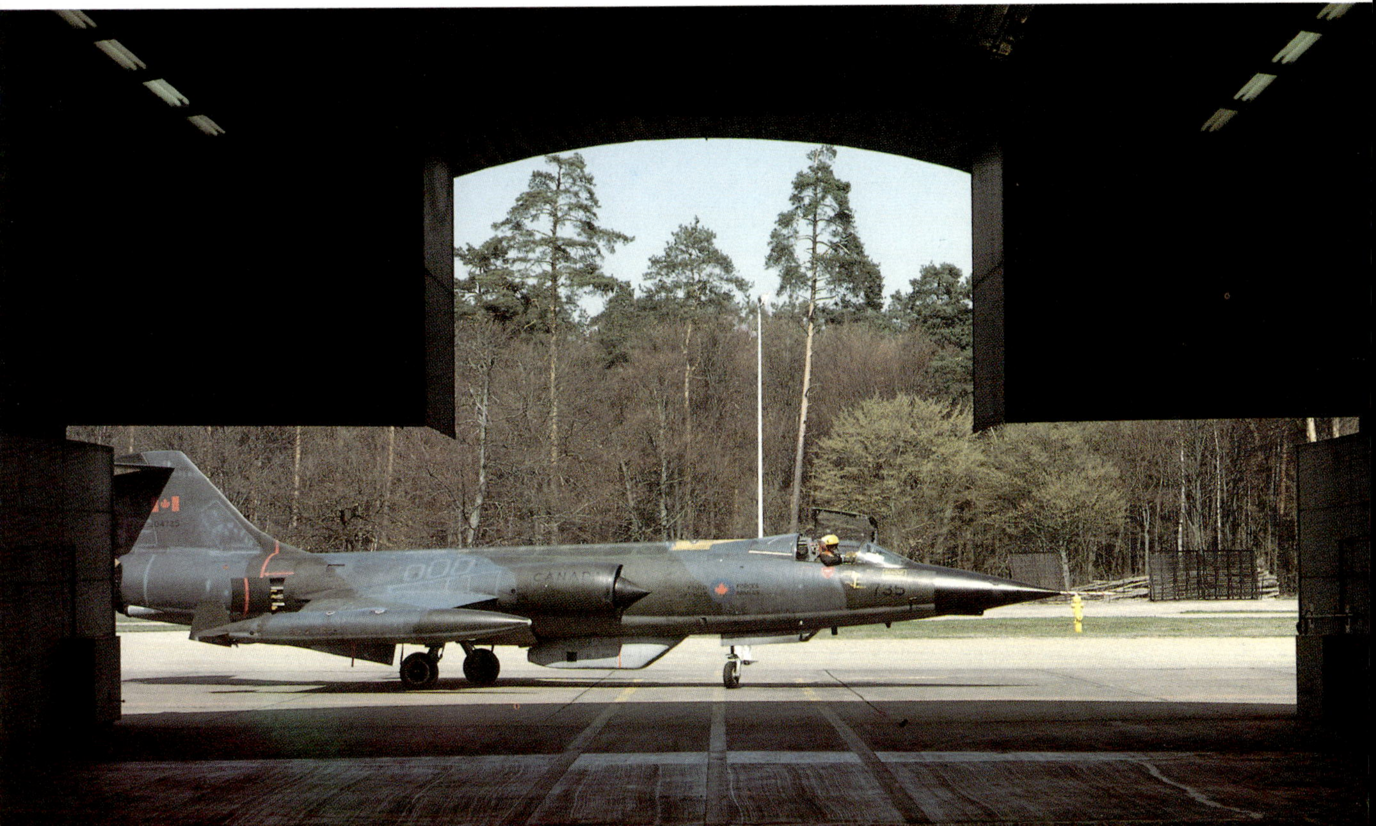

68. Canada received 38 CF-104D dual-seaters from Lockheed, the bulk of which went on to serve with No. 6 OTU, later to adopt the title 417 Squadron at CFB Cold Lake. This splendid night-time shot of 104651 undergoing engine runs in wintry conditions in Alberta epitomises the magic of the F-104. (Canadian Armed Forces)

▲ 69

69. The 'missile with a man in it': a Canadair-built CF-104, 104770, flown by a No. 439 Squadron pilot, formates over southern Germany in April 1984 during Exercise 'Jolly Rabbit'. The Starfighter was to become a legend in its own time without achieving a great deal other than adverse publicity.

70. The Canadians created some of the most striking F-104 colour schemes. Any excuse was always a good one, and this photograph shows one of No. 421 Squadron's various 'Coke Can' designs. This particular scheme was adopted for a visit of the 'Red Indians' to their Second World War home at Egerton, England, in 1982. (Canadian Armed Forces)

▼ 70

71. Although the operational squadrons with 1 CAG adopted commemorative schemes from time to time, No. 417 Squadron at Cold Lake, by virtue of its ever-changing complement, was never so blessed. However, with its impending disbandment in early 1983 the squadron saw fit to produce this tasteful design, viewed here against a typical Cold Lake range area and the golf balls of Primrose Lake radar station. (Canadian Armed Forces)

72. Canadair, as well as producing 200 CF-104s, also constructed 140 F-104Gs for MAP customers. One country to benefit from this line was Denmark, which was to receive 25 such aircraft. Intended to equip two units, *Esk 723* and *726* at Aalborg, the 25 airframes were really insufficient. Shown here is R-754 of *Esk 726*, in 'clean' configuration at RAF Coltishall during May 1982. (Author)

72▼

▲ 73

▲ 74 ▼ 75

73. With the adoption of the former Canadian machines in September 1971, Denmark was to operate 51 F-104s over the period 1965–1986, during which time twelve were lost in accidents. This was a very low attrition rate, a phrase not generally associated with the Starfighter. At the time of their retirement in April 1986 the former MAP airframes were scheduled to pass to Turkey, whilst the former Canadian machines will no doubt find their way into various ground roles; for example, RT-654 of *Esk 723*, seen here at Ramstein Air Base in August 1979, has been retired to Vaerløse Air Base as a technical training aid. (Author)

74. Norway, like Denmark, adopted the F-104, although for reasons of funding its order was cut back to 21 airframes (nineteen F-104Gs and two TF-104Gs) when it was discovered that more F-5s could be procured for the same price. The first aircraft went to *331 Skv* at Bodo and received the squadron codes 'FN': depicted here is the Lockheed-built Starfighter 62-12238/'FN-N' at Ypenburg in May 1972. This airframe still serves in Norway as a technical training aid. (Via G. B. Rhodes)

75. Both the TF-104Gs bought by Norway were eventually to crash, 62-12264 on 19 November 1970 at Aalborg, Denmark, and

62-12263 (shown) on 4 April 1985 after its transfer to Turkey in July 1981. Norway also acquired two former Luftwaffe TF-104Gs from Luke Air Force Base and one of these, 63-13627, also crashed. (Author)

76. As with all other recipients of MAP funded F-104s, Norway eventually transferred her Starfighters to Turkey: here seven ex-*331 Skv* examples, both Canadair- and Lockheed-produced, await collection at RAF Sculthorpe by Turkish Air Force crews, July 1981. Aircraft 62-12232, in the foreground, now serves with No. 9 Wing Turkish Air Force, still resplendent in its Norwegian air defence grey colour scheme. (Author)

77. In similar vein to Denmark, Norway was able to rectify its earlier error by buying 22 redundant CAF airframes in May 1973 to re-equip *334 Skv*. This purchase consisted of nineteen CF-104s and three CF-104Ds but, unlike Denmark's aircraft, they remained in their original configuration. *334 Skv*'s F-104s were to outlast *331*'s by nearly two years and the airframes were to retain their olive colour scheme. CF-104 890 is seen here arriving at the IAT, Greenham Common, June 1979. (Milslides)

77▼

▲ 78

▲ 79

78. Probably the last visit to the UK by a Norwegian Starfighter occurred when CF-104D 637 stopped overnight at Alconbury on 21–22 April 1982. The aircraft is seen here departing in the early morning mist. (Author)

79. Also from Canadair came the majority of the aircraft supplied to Spain, the country with one of the briefest associations with the Starfighter and consequently the only one not to incur any attrition. All the Spanish aircraft were supplied under MAP funding and were subsequently returned to the US Air Force for onward delivery to Greece and Turkey. Here 32715, of *335 Mira* Royal Hellenic Air Force, is seen at Volkel, the Netherlands, in July 1980, the aircraft having previously been C8-1 of the Spanish Air Force. (Author)

80. Greece was to receive 36 F-104s under MAP, the first of which was delivered in April 1964 to *335 Mira, 114 Ptx.*, which by the end of that year was to accumulate 1,000 accident-free hours on the type. The bulk of the Greek airframes came from the Canadair production line, including 62-12314 seen here at the AMI base at Cameri during the 1980 Tiger Meet. (Author)

81. Very rarely do Greek Starfighters venture far afield, except on the occasional NATO exchange visit and to the Tiger Meet in which *335 Mira* fortunately participates. Depicted here is TF-104G 62-2278 at the 1974 meet in Bitburg; this particular machine is another former Spanish example and is probably the most widely travelled Greek F-104. (Author)

◄ **81**

▲82

82. A 'vic' of MAP F-104Gs from *114 Ptx*. photographed over the Greek olive groves. (Royal Hellenic Air Force)

83. Turkey, the other MAP recipient in AF South, commissioned two F-104 squadrons within 9 Wing at Murted. The aircraft were a mixture of Lockheed- and Canadair-built machines which were later to be supplemented by former Spanish Air Force Starfighters. TF-104G 62-2279/9-279 was one of these and the sister to that supplied to Greece; it is depicted here at Cameri Air Base, Italy, in 1981. (Giuseppe Candiani)

84. Following its original buy, Turkey was to start a large re-equipment programme with the Starfighter: she initially acquired 22 F-104S models from Aeritalia which were again assigned to 9 Wing, Murted, and this purchase was to be followed by that of virtually everybody's surplus airframes. F-104S 6903 is seen here on the ramp at Lechfeld during 1981. (Author)

85. Turkey went on to receive some 100 former Luftwaffe, 40 Canadian, thirteen Norwegian, seventeen Belgian and 55 Dutch Starfighters, yet the only aircraft that seem to have been retired are the ageing F-100s! The aircraft continue to be operated in their original colours until a major overhaul is deemed necessary, during which they seem to be adopting a similar scheme to that adorning the former Luftwaffe F-104s. The ex-Klu F-104G 8272 is shown here departing from Leeuwarden on delivery to Turkey during September 1980, still sporting its Dutch serial. (Author's Collection)

86. The final recipient of MAP-funded F-104s was Taiwan, formerly Formosa, whose aircraft are also the most elusive. A single squadron of F-104As to equip 28 Squadron was accepted initially, and this was later supplemented by about 50 Lockheed- and Canadair-built -G models, which still serve with 5 Wing at Ching Chuan Kang Air Base. The aircraft display both the USAF serial and a CNAF serial, as demonstrated here on TF-104G 61-3026/4149 at Clark Air Base in the Philippines. (D. L. Jay)

▼83

84 ▲

85 ▲   86 ▼

▲ 87

87. Mitsubishi at Komaki/Nagoya produced some 210 F-104Js under licence for the Japanese Air Self-Defence Force, although the first JASDF Starfighter, 26-8501, was built by Lockheed (making its first flight from Burbank on 1 July 1961) and was then dismantled and shipped to Komaki, where it was re-assembled and flew on 8 March 1962. The F-104s equipped seven squadrons between October 1962 and March 1966. Depicted here is 76-8689, of *202 Hikotai, 5 Kokudan*, whilst under maintenance at Nyuta-baru Air Base. (Author)

88. *203 Hikotai, 2 Kokudan*, based at Chitose Air Base, Sapporo, displays the symbolic bear — a representative wild animal in Hokkaido — within its markings. The unit was formed in 1966 but with the Starfighter now retired from front-line service its current equipment is the F-15 Eagle. In this photograph F-104Js 36-8542 and 46-8641 complete a PAR approach to a full stop at Chitose in October 1976. (Author)

89. F-104DJs were allocated to each unit for proficiency training,

and this impressive line of *203 Hikotai* F-104s includes both F-104DJ and F-104J versions. The unit markings are, as is usually the case within the JASDF, very cleverly devised: the shape to the left of the marking is a geometrical figure '2', whilst to the right is clearly a figure '3'; the stomach of the bear forms the '0', and read together the three parts make up the number '203'. (G. B. Rhodes)

90. Although US forces were quick to learn from the experience of the Vietnam War, it took several years for other countries to adopt some of the fighter training programmes that were so successfully introduced by such units as Top Gun. However, the problem facing many air arms was the lack of dissimilar forces against which they could train. Japan, like Sweden, therefore adopted a policy of painting clearly visible markings on aircraft so that, when air combat missions were flown, identification of 'friend' or 'foe' was more easily maintained. This *203 Hikotai* F-104J, 56-8673, is wearing red and white ACM markings during in a fighter meet at Komatsu in October 1979. (Hideki Nagakubo via R. F. Dorr)

▼ 88

26-5003
46-8600
600
574
46-8574
541
36-8541
581
201

89▲ 90▼

203
328
362
014
56-8663
663
56-8666
46-8641
56-8673
673

▲ 91

91. In the 1980s, in accordance with revised thinking on air defence schemes and towards the end of the F-104's service in Japan, Starfighters, along with F-4s and F-15s, began to adopt a number of varied colour schemes. F-104J 76-8689, of *203 Hikotai* at Komatsu in June 1982, appears in more conservative paintwork, however. (Akira Watanabe)

92. A four-ship F-104J formation from *204 Hikotai, 5 Kokudan*, at the annual air day at Tsuiki Air Base in November 1976. That year saw the last occasion on which 32 F-86s flew past in formation before 'attacking' the base. (Author)

93. F-104DJ 26-5005 and F-104J 56-8675 prepare to leave Tsuiki Air Base whilst a KV-107 from the rescue flight acts as plane guard. No. 5 Wing served as the operational training unit for the Starfighter in Japan, and *202* and *204 Hikotai* displayed the same

▼ 92

design of markings; *204*'s, which was blue, clearly shows the roman numeral 'V', for *5 Kokudan*. (Author)

94. The serialising system adopted by the JASDF is, at first glance, confusing, but in fact it can be understood very easily. The first digit denotes the year of procurement (e.g. '4' = 1964) and the next two denote the type ('6' = fast jet, then '8' = all-weather jet fighter); the fourth, fifth, and sixth digits are the aircraft's basic number. Here *204 Hikotai* F-104J, serial 46-8614, is seen on approach to Nyuta-baru Air Base in November 1983 displaying an overall grey colour scheme. (Toshiki Kudo)

95. Representative of the great variety of colour schemes adopted by the JASDF in the 1980s, F-104DJ 26-5004 appears here in a very dark splinter scheme which effectively breaks up the aircraft's outline whilst maintaining *204 Hikotai* markings. (Toshiki Kudu)

96. Most JASDF fighter units are on 'alert' status and, given the close proximity of the USSR, record a high number of interceptions. In 1976 alert 'barns' did not exist at Komatsu (although they have since been constructed) and the aircraft merely occupied one corner of the ramp. Here F-104J 36-8531 of *205 Hikotai* does its duty, displaying the tail markings of a stylized 'six', indicating 6 *Kokudan*. (Author)

97. In May 1978 *205 Hikotai* revised its markings, although the original stylized 'six' was still carried, just aft of the jet intake. The new markings seen here on 46-8580 also incorporate the shape of the Ishikawa Profective, where Komatsu Air Base is located, and the Kanji character pronounced 'Ishi' (as in Ishikawa). (G. B. Rhodes)

98. Aircraft 36-8540, of *206 Hikotai*, in the attractive natural metal finish so often associated with JASDF F-104s. Flying from Hyakuri, close to the city of Mito and also the nearest fighter base to Tokyo, these Starfighters portray a stylized 'seven', for 7 *Kokudan*, and a Kairakuen plum flower, signifying the famous Japanese plum garden located in Mito. This unit operated Starfighters from 1966 to 1978 and then moved on to Phantoms. (Author)

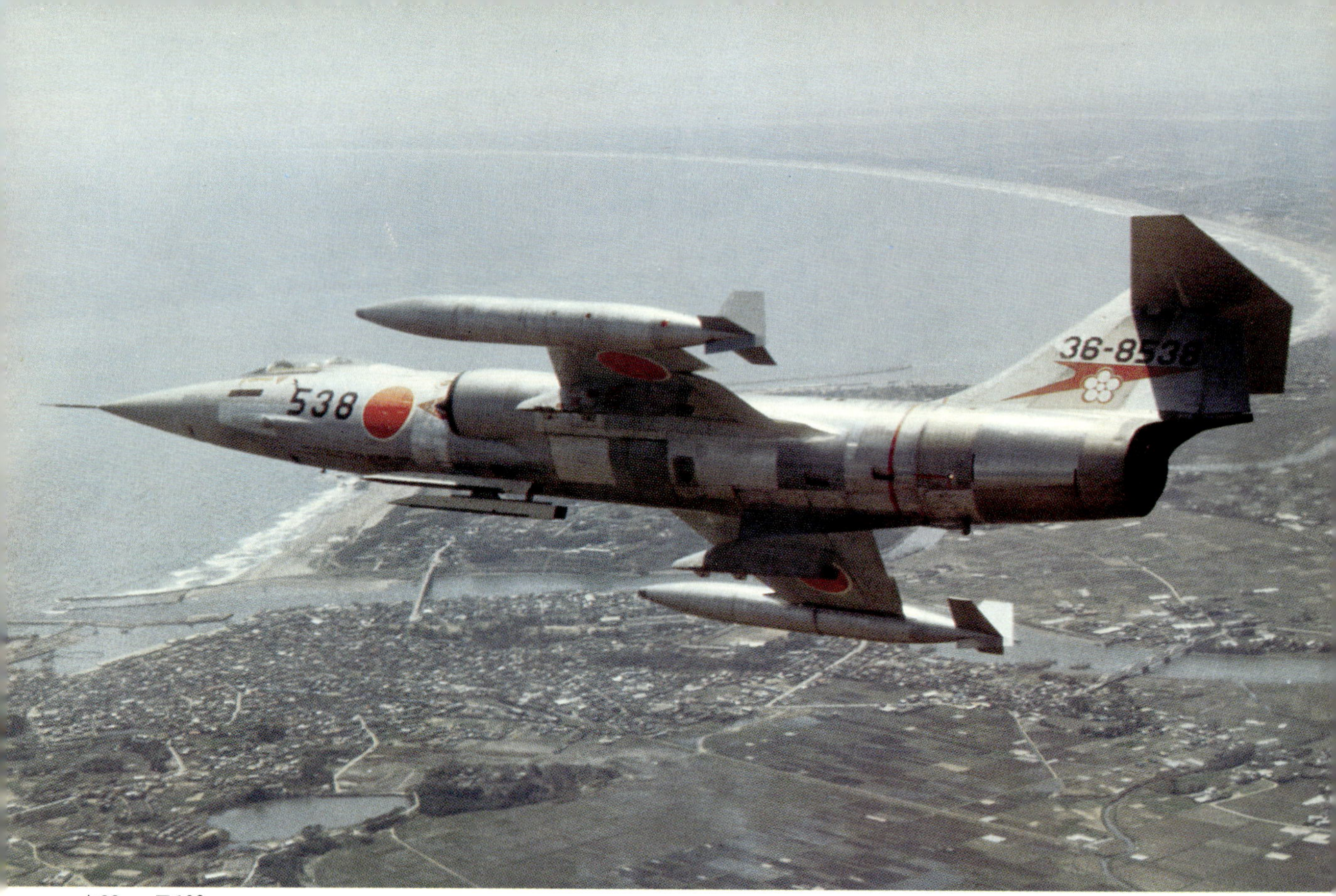

▲99 ▼100

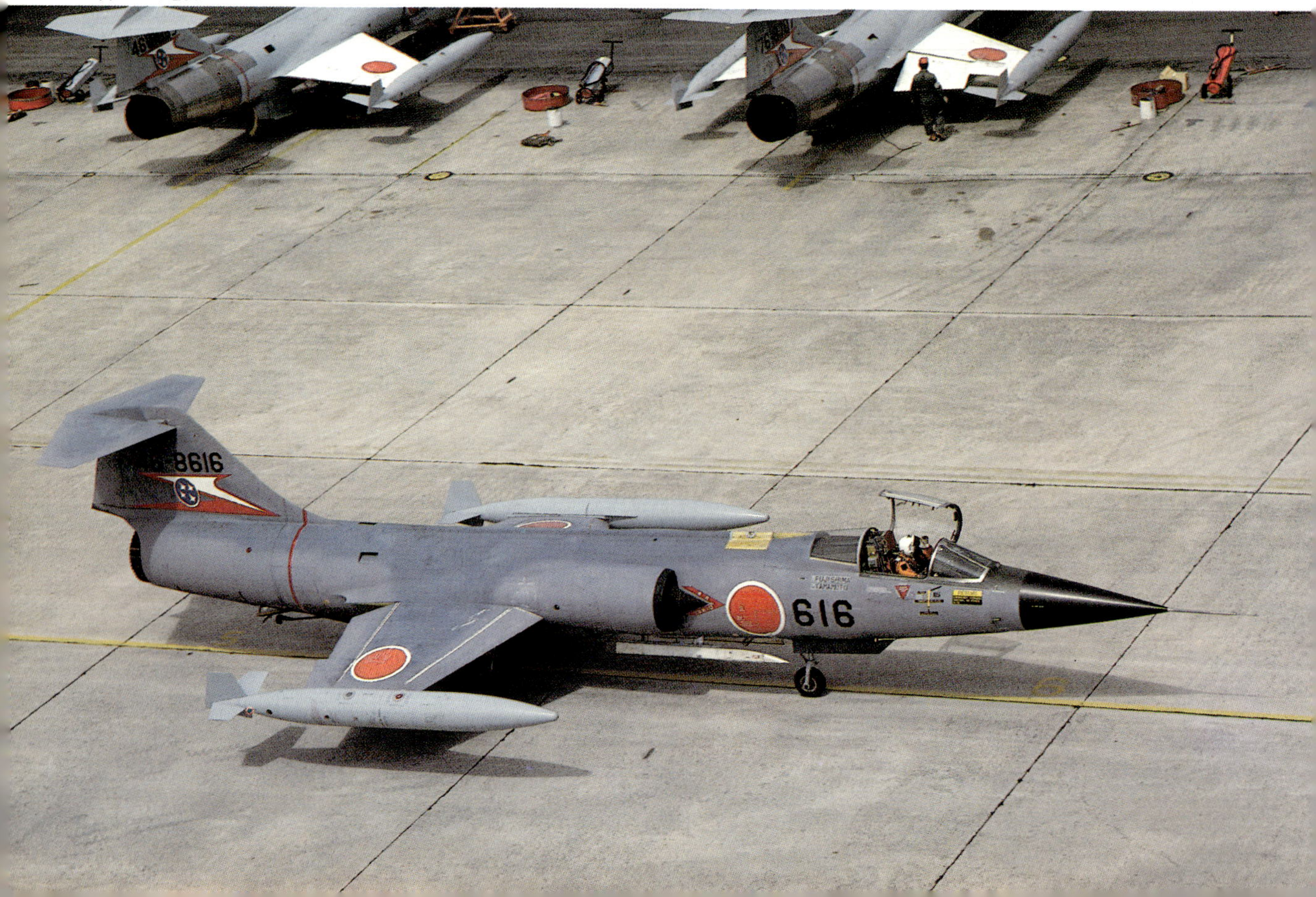

99. Before the introduction of the F-4EJ, 7 *Kokudan* at Hyakuri Air Base operated two *Hikotai*, the 206th and 207th, the latter transferring to Naha Air Base on Okinawa in 1972. Seen here is F-104J 36-8538 of *207 Hikotai* over the northern part of Tokyo Bay shortly before the unit's transfer south. The aircraft displays the stylized 'seven' in red instead of the blue of its sister-unit. (JASDF via R. F. Dorr)

100. The only Starfighter unit within the JASDF to operate its aircraft in anything other than natural metal finish, *207 Hikotai* was located at Naha Air Base on the island of Okinawa. The aircraft were mostly painted in a light grey polyurethane finish as an anti-corrosion measure but this example, 46-8616, seen in 1982, wears one of the many air defence schemes devised during this period. (Toshiki Kudo)

101. F-104DJ 26-5003, of *207 Hikotai*, in the grey colours that were sported after its move from Hyakuri to Naha in 1972. The tail marking is again cleverly devised: the red marks are a stylized 'two', the blue ellipse can be read as 'zero', and the white portion outlined in red is a stylized 'seven'. The four white stars in the ellipse represent the constellation Southern Cross, which in Japan can only be seen from Okinawa. (Author)

102. The final JASDF user of the Starfighter is the Air Proving Wing (APW) at Gifu, which has several examples on strength for test purposes. Gifu has also been turned into the final resting place for Japanese F-104s. Many examples now lie in storage awaiting the outcome of the drone programme; if successful, the F-104 will, for the second time in its career, find itself serving in this role. (Author)

▲103

▲104 ▼105

103. Italy has been left until last in this book because the final F-104 derivative was produced by Aeritalia at Turin. The F-104G was the most widely used variant, and the -J was essentially built to the same standard. Under the initial European consortium arrangements Fiat was to produce 200 airframes for the AMI (Italian Air Force), Luftwaffe and Klu, but only *3° Stormo* now flies the -G variant. MM6585/3-01 depicted here at Villafranca-Verona displays the markings of *18° Gruppo*. (G. B. Rhodes)

104. Italian Starfighters utilized their Fiat (and later the Aeritalia) construction numbers as serials, prefixed by 'MM', for *Matricola Militare*, and this aircraft also displays the unit code '3' followed by the individual *Gruppo* number: MM6633/3-26 thus belongs to *3° Stormo, 132° Gruppo*, which was allocated the codes 19 to 35. This example, photographed at Villafranca in 1983, is an RF-104G converted by Fiat; the camera bay can be seen behind the nose wheel bay. (Author's Collection)

105. The third unit at Villafranca is *28° Gruppo*, which operates standard F-104G models equipped with the Orpheus

reconnaissance pod; the aircraft shown, MM6514/3-42, is landing at RAF Cottesmore, May 1982. *28° Gruppo* may well be the first unit to re-equip with AMX. (Author)

106. Italy was the only country to attempt to upgrade the Starfighter's performance and medium-altitude effectiveness, and the F-104S all-weather fighter was configured with two AIM-7 Sparrow Mk.3 radar-seeking missiles in addition to a maximum of four AIM-9 Sidewinders. Four additional stores stations were incorporated for the strike role, and the aircraft's gross weight rose to 31,000lb. This is F-104S MM6937, the 192nd example built, in the markings of *4° Stormo*. (Author)

107. Grosetto is home to *4° Stormo, 9° Gruppo*, operating the F-104S, and also to *20° Gruppo*, which, flying TF-104Gs, acts as the operational conversion unit. Until recently only *9° Gruppo* operated with the code number '4', and MM6706/4-1 is seen here landing at Twenthe Air Base, Holland, during a NATO exchange with No. 315 Squadron Klu in October 1985. (Author)

▲ 108

▲ 109 ▼ 110

108. *20° Gruppo*, which shares Grosetto with *9° Gruppo*, operates the entire complement of TF-104Gs purchased by the AMI although the aircraft are, on occasions, loaned out to other units for proficiency checks. The unit was unique in operating in *20° Gruppo* markings whilst tenant to *4° Stormo*, although during 1985 the aircraft became an integral part of the *Stormo* and the aircraft were recoded. TF-104G MM54237/20-12 is seen here having just landed at RAF Alconbury. (Author)

109. Originally *20° Gruppo* operated only TF-104Gs, but as single-seaters became available in the early 1980s, owing to the introduction of the Tornado, several were taken on charge to help relieve the burden on the two-seaters in both the conversion and proficiency roles. MM6588/20-28 depicted here had earlier seen service with both *5°* and *3° Stormos* and is now stored at Villafranca-Verona. (Author's Collection)

110. The -S model Starfighter became standard with AMI, eventually equipping ten *Gruppi*. The first F-104Ss were converted -Gs, MM6658 and MM6660, the work having been carried out by Lockheed at Palmdale, California, and the first flight taking place in December 1966; the first production F-104S entered service with *22° Gruppo* on 9 June 1969 in the interceptor role. MM6714/5-45 is depicted here taxiing out at RAF Coningsby whilst on a NATO exchange with No. 29 Squadron in July 1985. (Author)

111. MM6705/5-43, also seen whilst on exchange at Coningsby, displays the 5° *Stormo* badge on the fin, 'Diana Cacciatrice' (Diana the Hunter) in white, whilst on the fuselage just aft of the engine intake is the 23° *Gruppo* badge, a yellow triangle with a black greyhound over a red missile. 23° *Gruppo* serves as an interceptor unit whilst its sister-squadron at Rimini, 102° *Gruppo*, is a tactical squadron. (Author)

112. In Starfighter days Italy's only dedicated nuclear strike unit was 154° *Gruppo*, under 6° *Stormo* at Ghedi, although this has now been joined by 155° *Gruppo*, both operating the Tornado. MM6510/6-01, sporting the 6° *Stormo* red devil emblem on the fin, is depicted here on the taxiway at Volkel in the Netherlands, October 1967. (Author)

113. Always noted for its impressive performance and especially its ultra-low approaches, Starfighters also required incredibly high landing speeds, as shown here by MM6553/6-21. This airframe was to see service with only the 3° and 6° *Stormos* before crashing on 11 July 1979. (Author)

111▲

112▲   113▼

59

▲114 ▼115

116 ▲

114. Visits to the UK by Italian Starfighters have always been rare and opportunities to photograph them very few. However, MM6783/9-36, of *10° Gruppo, 9° Stormo*, is caught here in the early morning light at the 'last chance' point at RAF Alconbury, April 1978. One of the many problems affecting the Italian Starfighters' ability to reach Britain was their poor transponders, coupled with French air traffic control's normal restrictive practices. (Author)

115. The ultimate interceptor — although its endurance was somewhat limited. The F-104S depicted here, MM6774/36-0 of *12° Gruppo, 36° Stormo*, shows its maximum intercept load of four

AIM-9 Sidewinder heat-seeking missiles and two AIM-7 Sparrow radar-seeking missiles, plus two pylon tanks. (Author's Collection)

116. The sister-unit to *12° Gruppo* at Gioia del Colle in Southern Italy is *156° Gruppo*, whose aircraft are easily identifiable by the yellow lightning flash through the *36° Stormo* badge as opposed to the green of *12° Gruppo*. This aircraft, coded 36-30, is at the end of its landing run, with braking parachute streamed; the foreground shows the normal unkempt condition of Italian airfields. (Massimo Gori)

▲117

117. MM6789/36-42, also of *156° Gruppo*, photographed whilst on detachment to RAF Bruggen, West Germany. *156° Gruppo* was the second Italian fighter unit to convert to the Tornado. (Author's Collection)

118. *22° Gruppo* began conversion to the F-104S on June 1969, detaching to Cameri for the three-month period, although it was not until the end of January 1972 that the unit became fully operational with the type. Today, *22°* is the only squadron resident at Istrana Air Base. MM6850/51-20 is shown being towed to the 'alert' facility and is armed with an AIM-7 Sparrow missile; the pipe-smoking scarecrow of the *Gruppo* can be seen on the intake whilst the *51° Stormo* cat appears on the tail. (Author's Collection)

119. *22° Gruppo's* sister-unit at Istrana was *155° Gruppo*, which replaced *23° Gruppo* within the *51° Stormo* during 1974, having previously served with the now-disbanded *50° Stormo*. MM6788/51-33, wearing its panther emblem, is seen here outside the maintenance hangar at Istrana in 1981. The unit has now converted to the Tornado and moved to Ghedi under *6° Stormo*. (Author's Collection)

120. MM6764/53-07, of the *21° Gruppo*, banks hard into the approach during the 1980 Tiger Meet at Cameri. The *53° Stormo* was formed on 1 April 1967, thus ending *21° Gruppo's* autonomy; the unit then equipped with the F-104G, converting to the F-104S during 1970, and is now, by virtue of the Tiger aquaintance, the most travelled AMI Starfighter unit. (Author)

121. Photographed over the Mediterranean, on a not particularly clear day, MM6850/53-10 flies high, armed with an AIM-7 Sparrow. While maintaining its autonomy at Cameri the unit originally coded its aircraft with the prefix '21', and although it is still the only F-104 unit to be based there it had to fall in line and adopt the *Stormo* code in 1967. (Giuseppe Candiani)

▼118

119▲

120▲　121▼

▲122

▲123 ▼124

122. Unlike most other AMI bases, Cameri does not enjoy the benefits of hardened aircraft shelters and its aircraft still operate from a flight line. MM6933/53-14, seen here in August 1979 at Cameri, lacks the normal *Gruppo* badge on the intake but displays the *53° Stormo* scimitar on its fin. (Author)

123. One of the Italian F-104 units less frequently seen is *Reporto Sperimentale di Volo* (*RSV*); located at Practica di Mare, it is tasked with research and development and has on strength several examples of the Starfighter, including the prototype F-104S. MM6848/RS-04 is seen here on the ramp at Cameri in 1979 and is thought still to be operational. (Giuseppe Candiani)

124. The final photograph in this book shows, appropriately, the last Starfighter to be built, number 2581. The Italians originally planned to buy 205 F-104s, but Aeritalia produced an additional twenty airframes in anticipation of a follow-on order from Turkey which in the event failed to materialize. However, with the loss of MM6766 before delivery to the Air Force, one of these airframes was completed as a replacement, and MM6946/5-06 is thus the Starfighter that nearly wasn't; it is seen here whilst serving with the *102° Gruppo, 5° Stormo*, during a NATO exchange visit at RAF Bentwaters in August 1983. (Author)